HUGO WOLF

Spanish and Italian Songbooks

DOVER PUBLICATIONS, INC.
NEW YORK

Bibliographical Note

This Dover edition, first published in 1989 and reprinted in 2010, is a republication of two editions originally published by C. F. Peters, Leipzig, n.d. [c. 1904]: *Spanisches Liederbuch nach Heyse und Geibel für eine Singstimme und Klavier* and *Italienisches Liederbuch nach Paul Heyse für eine Singstimme und Klavier.* The song texts have been newly translated, and a glossary prepared, for this edition.

International Standard Book Number

ISBN-13: 978-0-486-26156-0
ISBN-10: 0-486-26156-5

Manufactured in the United States by Courier Corporation
26156507   2014
www.doverpublications.com

Contents

Alphabetical List of Song Openings

Translations of Song Texts
Spanish Songbook

SPIRITUAL SONGS

1. *Nun bin ich dein*

Now I am yours,
flower of all flowers,
and I sing only
your praises hourly;
I shall be eager
to dedicate myself
to you and your silent suffering.
Exquisite Lady,
on you I fix all my hopes,
my innermost being
is always open to you.
Come and release me
from the Evil One's spell,
which has so harshly affected me!
You star of the sea,
you haven of bliss,
from whom in their pain
the injured have gained their cure,
before I die,
look down from on high,
you queen of the sun!
Never can the fullness
of your mercy run dry;
you help to victory
those burdened with shame.
To nestle against you,
to lie at your feet,
heals all affliction and harm.
I suffer harsh
and well-deserved punishment;
I so fear
that I will soon sleep the sleep of death.
Come,
and across the sea,
oh, guide me to my haven.

2. *Die du Gott gebarst, du Reine*

You who bore God, you pure one,
and alone
loosed us from our chains,
make me joyful, I who weep,
for only your
grace and mercy may redeem us.
Lady, I turn entirely to you,
so that this pain and this fear
may come to an end,
so that death may find me fearless,
and the light
of the heavenly meadows not blind me.
Since you were born immaculate,
chosen
for realms of eternal glory,
although I am veiled in sorrows,
yet I am
not lost if you wish to save me.

3. *Nun wandre, Maria*

Now journey on, Mary, now journey forth.
Already the cocks are crowing and the place is near.
Now journey on, beloved, my jewel,
and soon we will be in Bethlehem.
Then will you rest so well and slumber there.
Already the cocks are crowing and the place is near.
I see well, my lady, that your strength is waning;
ah, it can hardly bear your sufferings.
Courage! we will surely find lodging there;
already the cocks are crowing and the place is near.
If your delivery were only over, Mary,
I would give a good reward for the glad tidings.
I would give away the donkey here in exchange!
Already the cocks are crowing, come! the place is near.

4. *Die ihr schwebet um diese Palmen*

You who hover around these palms
in night and wind,
you holy angels, calm the treetops! my child is sleeping.
You palms of Bethlehem in the roar of the wind,
how can you whistle so angrily today!
Oh, do not roar that way! be still, bend softly and gently;
calm the treetops! my child is sleeping.
The heavenly child endures hardship;
ah, how tired he's become with the sorrow of earth.
Ah, now in sleep, gently soothed, his pain melts away;
calm the treetops! my child is sleeping.
Furious cold whistles down;
with what can I cover the little child's limbs!
O all you angels who rove winged in the wind,
calm the treetops! my child is sleeping.

5. *Führ mich, Kind, nach Bethlehem*

Lead me, child, to Bethlehem!
you, my God, you would I see.
Who could succeed, who,
in journeying to you without you!
Shake me to rouse me,
call me and I will walk on;
give me your hand to guide me,
that I may set out on my way.
That I may gaze on Bethlehem,
there to see my God.
Who could succeed, who,
in journeying to you without you!
From the grave illness of sin
I am sluggish and weighed down with gloom.
If you will not come to my aid,
I must stumble, I must stagger.
Guide me to Bethlehem,
you, my God, you would I see.
Who could succeed, who,
in journeying to you without you!

6. *Ach, des Knaben Augen*

Ah, the boy's eyes
look so beautiful and clear,
and something shines from them
that wins my whole heart.
If he would only look with his sweet
eyes into my own!
if he then saw his image therein,
perhaps he would greet me lovingly.
And so I give myself completely,
only to serve his eyes,
because something shines from them
that wins my whole heart.

7. *Mühvoll komm' ich und beladen*

Full of cares and weighed down I come,
accept me, you refuge of grace!
See, I come in hot tears
with humble gestures,
all black with the dust of earth.
Only you can make me
white as lambs' fleece.
You will truly erase the injuries
of him who, contrite, embraces you;
take then, Lord, from me my burden,
full of cares and weighed down I come.
Let me kneel pleading before you,
that I, on thy feet,
may pour spikenard fragrance and tears,
like the woman whom you forgave,
until guilt dissipates like smoke.
You who invited the thief,
"This very day you will be in the realm of Eden!"
accept me, you refuge of grace!

8. *Ach, wie lang die Seele schlummert!*

Ah, how long the soul slumbers!
It is time for it to rouse itself.
It sleeps so heavily and fearfully
that it could be taken for dead,
since it was overcome by that intoxication
which befell it through drinking the poison of sin.
But now the light it longed for
shines dazzlingly on its eyes;
it is time for it to rouse itself.
If at first it seems deaf
to the sweet choir of the angels,
it will nevertheless listen timidly to the sound above
and hear God crying in the form of a small child.
Since after a long night of slumber,
such a day of grace smiles upon it,
it is time for it to rouse itself.

9. *Herr, was trägt der Boden hier*

Lord, what does the earth bear here,
that you water so bitterly?
"Thorns, beloved heart, for me,
and for you an adornment of flowers."
Ah, where such brooks run,
will a garden thrive there?
"Yes, and know this! Garlands
most varied are plaited therein."
O my Lord, for whose adornment
do they wind the garlands? Speak!
"Those of thorns are for me,
those of flowers I give to you."

10. *Wunden trägst du mein Geliebter*

Wounds you bear, my beloved,
and they cause you pain.
If only I could bear them instead of you, I!
Lord, who dares thus to color
your brow with blood and sweat?
"These marks are the price
for winning you, O soul.
From the wounds I must die,
because I have loved you so greatly."
If only, Lord, I could bear them for you,
since they are wounds that give death.
"If this song moves you, my child,
you may call them wounds that give life:
not one of them was inflicted
from which life does not flow for you."
Ah, how, in heart and mind,
your torment hurts me!
"Harsher still would I bear gladly
with true courage to win you;
since only he knows truly how to woo
who dies of the heat of love."
Wounds you bear, my beloved,
and they cause you pain;
if only I could bear them instead of you, I!

WORLDLY SONGS

1. *Klinge, klinge, mein Pandero*

Ring, ring, my tambourine,
yet my heart is thinking of something else.
If you, merry thing, understood
my torment and felt it,
every note that you uttered
would lament my pain.
In the dance's spinning and bowing
I wildly strike the beat of the round dance,
only to still the thoughts
that remind me of my pain.
Ah, gentlemen, then while whirling
often my heart feels like bursting
and my singing becomes a cry of anguish,
since my heart is thinking of something else.

2. *In dem Schatten meiner Locken*

In the shadow of my locks
my beloved fell asleep.
Should I wake him now? Ah, no!
Carefully I combed my curly
locks daily at dawn,
but my care is in vain,
since the wind dishevels them.
Locks' shadow, wind's bluster
put my beloved to sleep.
Should I wake him now? Ah, no!
I would have to hear how it distresses him
that he has already languished so long,
that these brown cheeks of mine
give and take life from him.
And he calls me his serpent
and he fell asleep with me anyway.
Should I wake him up now? Ah, no!

3. *Seltsam ist Juanas Weise*

Strange is Juana's manner.
If I am filled with sorrow,
if I sigh and say "today,"
"tomorrow" she says softly.
Gloomy is she when I am happy;
merrily she sings when I weep;
if I say that she seems sweet to me,
she says that she always shuns me.
Proofs of such cruelty
break my heart in sorrow;
if I sigh and say "today,"
"tomorrow" she says softly.
If I raise my eyelids,
she always manages to drop her gaze;
to make her look up at once,
I cast my own gaze down also.
If I praise her as a saint,
she calls me a demon, to quarrel,
if I sigh and say "today,"
"tomorrow" she says softly.
I find myself bereft of victory at once
if I praise my victory modestly;
If I hope for heavenly bliss
she prophesies hell for me.
Yes, so icy is her heart,
if she saw me dying of sorrow,
if she heard me still sighing "today,"
"tomorrow" she'd say softly.

4. *Treibe nur mit Lieben Spott*

Just make fun of love,
my beloved;
but the god of love will mock
you as well one day!
You may revel in mockery
as you please;
from woman comes
joy and sorrow for all of us.
If you are now too proud for love,
believe, oh believe:
love will still win you
as its prey,
if you mock my need,
my beloved;
the god of love will mock
you also one day!
Whoever is made of flesh and blood should consider
at all times:
Amor sleeps and, suddenly active,
he inflicts his wounds.
Just make fun of love,
my beloved;
but the god of love will mock
you as well one day!

5. *Auf dem grünen Balcon*

On the green balcony my sweetheart
looks at me through the grille.
With her eyes she gives a friendly wink,
with her finger she tells me: No!
Happiness, which never unwaveringly
follows young love here below,
has granted me a joy,
and even so I must still vacillate.
I hear flattery or scolding

when I come to her window shutter.
Always, as is the custom of girls,
there seeps into happiness a bit of pain.
With her eyes she gives a friendly wink,
with her finger she tells me: No!
Just how do they get along together in her,
her coldness, my heat?
Since in her my heaven lies,
I see gloom and brightness following after each other.
Into the wind go my complaints,
that the sweet little thing has not yet
wrapped her arms around mine;
but she puts me off so cunningly,
with her eyes she gives a friendly wink,
with her finger she tells me: No!

6. *Wenn du zu den Blumen gehst*

When you go to the flowers,
pluck the loveliest to adorn yourself.
Ah, when you stand in the garden,
you would have to pluck yourself.
All the flowers truly know
that you are fair beyond comparison.
And the flower that saw you
must lose its color and adornment.
More charming than roses are the kisses
that your mouth lavishes,
since the charm of the flowers ends
where your charm first begins.
When you go to the flowers,
pluck the loveliest to adorn yourself.
Ah, when you stand in the garden,
you would have to pluck yourself.

7. *Wer sein holdes Lieb verloren*

Whoever has lost his fair beloved
because he doesn't understand love,
better that he had never been born.
I lost her there in the garden,
when she was picking roses and blossoms.
Bright on her cheek glowed
shame and desire in fair adornment.
And of love she spoke to me;
but I, greatest of all fools,
had no answer for her;
would that I had never been born!
I lost her there in the garden,
when she spoke of the pains of love,
because I dared not tell her
how I was entirely hers.
Among the flowers she sank down;
but I, greatest of all fools,
did not even take advantage of that;
would that I had never been born!

8. *Ich fuhr über Meer*

I traveled over sea,
I strode over land,
happiness I found
never.
The others around,
how they rejoiced!
I never rejoiced!
For happiness I hunted,
from sorrows I suffered;
as a right I demanded

what love refused.
I hoped and dared,
but no love flourished for me,
and so I never saw it.
I bore without complaint
the sorrows, the evils,
and I thought how
the days follow one after the other.
The happy days,
how they hurry by!
I never overtook them!

9. *Blindes Schauen, dunkle Leuchte*

Blind looks, dark lights,
glory full of woe, perished life,
bad luck that I thought was good luck,
joyful weeping, pleasure full of trembling,
sweet bile, thirsty wetness,
war in peace everywhere:
Love, falsely you promised blessing,
while your curse frightened my sleep away.

10. *Eide, so die Liebe schwur*

Oaths that were sworn by love
are only feeble guarantors.
If love sits in judgment,
then, Señor, do not forget
that it has never acted according to right and duty,
always only according to favor.
Oaths that were sworn by love
are only feeble guarantors.
You will find sad people there
who pledge vows to one another
that vanish with the wind
like the flowers in the field.
Oaths that were sworn by love
are only feeble guarantors.
And as clerks at the desks
you see trifling thoughts.
Since their light little hands waver,
none of them writes a straight line for you.
Oaths that were sworn by love
are only feeble guarantors.
If the guarantors are present,
and everyone eager for the verdict,
they get the sentence ready;—
but there is no sign of carrying it out!
Oaths that were sworn by love
are only feeble guarantors.

11. *Herz verzage nicht geschwind*

Heart, do not despair too quickly,
since women will be women.
Let jealousy teach you to know them,
those who call themselves bright stars
and burn like fiery sparks.
Thus, do not despair too quickly,
since women will be women.
Do not let your mind be confused
when they coo sweet melodies;
they would like to soften you with cunning,
make you blind with intrigues;
since women will be women.
They are always in league together,

they fight boldly with their mouths,
they wish for what the moment won't allow,
they build castles in the wind;
since women will be women.
And their mind is so peculiar
that, if you praise the praiseworthy,
they rage against it with their mouth
even if their heart feels the same way you do;
since women will be women.

12. *Sagt, seid Ihr es, feiner Herr*

Tell me, are you the one, fine gentleman,
who very recently so prettily danced
and danced and sang?
Are you the one because of whom
no one else got a chance to speak?
You talked so big,
sang quite charmingly, without error.
Yes, you're the one, upon my life,
who got around us that way
and danced and sang.
Are you the one who at castanets
and song was never expert,
who never knew love,
who fled from the chains of women?
Yes, you're the one; but I'd like to bet
you have embraced many a love
and danced and sung.
Are you the one who praised
dance and songs so immoderately?
Are you the one who sat in the corner
and didn't stir his limbs?
Yes, you're the one, I recognize you,
who made us yawn
and danced and sang!

13. *Mögen alle bösen Zungen*

Let all evil tongues
always say what they like;
whoever loves me I love back,
and I love and am loved.
Wicked, wicked rumor
your tongues whisper mercilessly,
but I know they are merely
hungry for innocent blood.
Never shall it worry me,
gossip as much as you want;
whoever loves me I love back,
and I love and am loved.
Slandering is the only thing that's understood
by the one who has missed out on love and affection,
since he himself is so wretched
and no one woos and wants him.
That's why I think that love,
which they revile, gives me honor;
whoever loves me I love back,
and I love and am loved.
If I were made of stone and iron,
you might insist
that I should reject
lover's greeting and lover's plea.
But my little heart is now unfortunately
tender, as God grants us maidens;
whoever loves me I love back,
and I love and am loved.

14. *Köpfchen, Köpfchen, nicht gewimmert*

Little head, little head, don't fret,
stand your ground, stay cheerful;
place two good little pillars below to support you,
wholesomely constructed of patience!
Hope gleams
even as things get worse
and trouble you.
You must take nothing
to heart with worrying,
not even a fairytale
that makes your hair stand on end;
may God prevent that,
and the giant Christophor!

15. *Sagt ihm, dass er zu mir komme*

Tell him that he's to come to me,
since the more they scold me for it,
ah, the more my ardor grows!
Oh, nothing vanquishes
love on earth;
by their rebuking
it is only doubled.
The fury of those who envy it
may not threaten it,
since the more they scold me for it,
ah, the more my ardor grows!
They've locked me up
for days on end,
unceasingly
punished me with awful torments;
but I bear every trouble with lover's courage,
since the more they scold me for it,
ah, the more my ardor grows!
My tormentors
often say I should leave you,
but that will only make us
more united in our heart's embrace.
If I must fade away because of this,
dying for love is lovely,
and the more they scold me for it,
ah, the more my ardor grows!

16. *Bitt' ihn, o Mutter, bitte den Knaben*

Beg him, O Mother, beg the lad
to aim no more, because he's killing me.
Mother, O Mother, capricious Love
mocks and makes up to me, shuns me and lures me.
I saw two eyes last Sunday,
Wonder of heaven, disaster on earth.
What people say, O Mother, about basilisks,
my heart learned when I saw them.
Beg him, O Mother, beg the lad
to aim no more, because he's killing me.

17. *Liebe mir im Busen zündet einen Brand*

Love kindles a blaze in my bosom.
Water, dear Mother, before my heart burns up!
Do not punish the blind child
for my mistakes;
at first he cooled my soul
so mildly.
Then, ah! my folly
made it flare up swiftly;
water, dear Mother, before my heart burns up!
Ah, where is the flood

that will fight the fire?
for so great heat
the seas are too meager.
Since it does me good I weep constantly;
water, dear Mother, before my heart burns up!

18. *Schmerzliche Wonnen und wonnige Schmerzen*

Painful joys and joyful pains,
water in the eye and fire in the heart,
pride on the lips and sighs in the mind,
honey and gall at the same time is love.
Often, when a soul is separated from its body,
St. Michael will try to bear it up in peace.
But ah, the devil would like to devour it;
no one will give in, so it becomes a struggle.
Dear soul, tormented, in unquiet surges
you feel yourself pulled hither and thither,
upward and downward. In such turbulence
love hurls us between heaven and hell.
Ah, Mother, and at seventeen
I have suffered this fear and anxiety.
I then forswore it with tears of repentence;
ah, and already I'm in love again.

19. *Trau nicht der Liebe*

Trust not love, my dearest, beware!
It will make you weep where today you laughed.
And do you not see the moon's form fade?
No less is the foundation of happiness unsteady.
Then it soon takes revenge; and love, beware!
it will make you weep where today you laughed.
So just be on guard
against foolish pride!
The crickets may sing in May
in the wood;
then they die away, and love, beware!
it will make you weep where today you laughed.
Just where are you wandering?
Take this advice:
The child with the darts
has mischief in mind.
The days hurry by,
and love, beware!
it will make you weep where today you laughed.
It is not always clear,
it is not always dark,
joy's sparkle
fades so quickly.
A false companion
is Amor, beware!
he will make you weep where today you laughed.

20. *Ach im Maien war's*

Ah, in May it was, in May
when the warm breezes blow,
when people in love are accustomed
to go to their beloved.
I alone, I poor unhappy one,
lie in the dungeon languishing so,
and I see not when day breaks,
and I know not when night falls.
Only by a little bird was I able to tell,
which sang there outside in the springtime;
an archer killed it for me—
God give him the harshest thanks!

21. *Alle gingen, Herz, zur Ruh*

All have gone to their rest, heart,
all are sleeping except you.
Because hopeless care
frightens away slumber from your bed,
and your thoughts wander in silent
sorrow to their love.

22. *Dereinst, dereinst Gedanke mein*

One day, one day, my thoughts,
you will be at peace.
If the ardor of love won't let you be still,
in the cool earth you will sleep well;
there, without love and without suffering,
you will be at peace.
What you have not found in life
will be given to you when it has passed away.
Then, without wounds and without suffering,
you will be at peace.

23. *Tief im Herzen trag' ich Pein*

Deep in my heart I bear suffering,
outwardly I must be silent.
The cherished pain I hide
deep from the world's sight;
and only the soul feels it,
since the body deserves it not.
As the spark, free and bright,
hides itself in the flint,
I bear my suffering deep within.

24. *Komm, o Tod, von Nacht umgeben*

Come, O death, surrounded by night,
softly come to me,
that the desire to embrace you
not call me back to life.
Come just as the lightning strikes us
which the thunder does not announce
before it suddenly ignites
and deals the bolt with double force.
Therefore may you be granted me,
suddenly stilling my longing,
that the desire to embrace you
not call me back to life.

25. *Ob auch finstre Blicke glitten*

Even though dark glances were cast
by you, lovely darling,
still it cannot be denied me
that you have glanced at me.
No matter how the beam endeavored
to wound my breast,
is there a sorrow that the joy
of gazing on you does not richly outweigh?
And as mortally as my soul
has suffered from your anger,
still it cannot be denied me
that you have glanced at me.

26. *Bedeckt mich mit Blumen*

Cover me with flowers, I die for love.
That the breeze with its gentle wafting
not carry the sweet fragrance away from me, cover me!
Yet truly it is all the same,

breath of love or odor of flowers.
Of jasmine and white lilies
shall you here prepare my grave, I die.
And if you ask me, Why?
I say, From sweet torments of love.

27. *Und schläfst du, mein Mädchen*

And if you're sleeping, my sweetheart, up, open the door for
    me;
for the hour is come to journey from here.
And if you have no soles, don't put any on;
through rushing water runs our path.
Through the deep, deep water of the Guadalquivir;
for the hour is come to journey from here.

28. *Sie blasen zum Abmarsch*

They're playing for the departure, dear Mother.
My dearest must be going and leave me here alone!
In the sky the stars have hardly disappeared,
there yonder the infantry are already firing.
He hardly hears the sound, he laces up his pack,
away he marches,
my heart behind him.
My dearest must be going and leave me here alone!
I feel like a day
from which the sun has faded;
my sorrows may not
so soon recover.
I care about nothing,
I feel no more joy,
I only commune
with my suffering.
My dearest must be going and leave me here alone!

29. *Weint nicht, ihr Äuglein!*

Weep not, little eyes!
How can someone who kills by love so gloomily weep for
    jealousy?
Should whoever brings death long for it himself?
His smile overcomes that which defies his tears.
Weep not, little eyes!
How can someone who kills by love so gloomily weep for
    jealousy?

30. *Wer that deinem Füsslein weh?*

"Who hurt your little foot?
La Marioneta,
your heel white as snow?
La Marion!"
I'll tell you what makes me ill;
I don't want to keep a bit of it from you.
I went to the rosebush at night,
broke a rose from the branch;
stepped on a thorn on my way,
la Marioneta,
which penetrated to my heart,
la Marion.
I'll tell you all my suffering,
friend, and I won't lie to you:
I went into a wood alone
to pluck myself a lily;
a spine hurt me sharply there,
la Marioneta,
it was a sweet word of love,
la Marion.

I'll tell you honestly
my sickness, my wound:
into the garden I went today,
where the loveliest carnation grew;
a splinter injured me there,
la Marioneta,
it has bled and bled till now,
la Marion.
"Beautiful lady, if you desire,
I am a surgeon of good skill;
I will stop your wound so gently
that you will not even know it.
You will soon be recovered,
la Marioneta,
soon healed of all pain,
la Marion."

31. *Deine Mutter, süsses Kind*

Your mother, sweet child,
when she lay in childbirth,
heard the wind roaring.
And thus did she bear you
with a false, fickle mind.
If you have chosen a heart today,
you'll discard it tomorrow faithlessly.
But I will count among the fools
the man who reviles you for your faithlessness:
Your fate was against you;
because your mother, sweet child,
when she lay in childbirth,
heard the wind roaring.

32. *Da nur Leid und Leidenschaft*

Since only sorrow and passion
assail me in your custody,
I now offer my heart for sale.
Say, does anyone desire it?
If I should say how I value it,
three silver coins are not too much.
Never was it the wind's plaything,
it remained stubborn even when caught in the net.
But since need presses me,
I now offer my heart for sale,
I'll get rid of it to the highest bidder;
say, does anyone desire it?
Daily it grieves me in silence
and never gladdens me.
Now who offers? who'll give more?
Away with it and its silly whims!
that they are bad is clear;
still, I offer my heart for sale.
If it were happy, I'd be glad to keep it;
say, does anyone desire it?
If you buy it, I'll live without complaining;
whoever it pleases may have it.
Now who will buy? who wants to take it?
Each one say what he will give.
Once again before the hammer blow

I now offer my heart for sale,
so that people may decide—
say, does anyone desire it?
Now the first blow and the second,
and at the third I knock it down!
Good, then! May it give you happiness;
take it, my dearest, you!
With the glowing metal, brand it
at once with the mark of the slave;
for I make you a present of my heart
even if you have no desire to buy it.

33. *Wehe der, die mir verstrickte*

Woe to her who ensnared my beloved!
Woe to her who ensnared him!
Ah, the first man that I loved
was captured in Seville.
My dearly beloved,
woe to her who ensnared him!
He was captured in Seville
with the chain of my locks.
My dearly beloved,
woe to her who ensnared him!
Woe to her!

34. *Geh, Geliebter, geh jetzt!*

Go, beloved, go now!
See, the morning breaks.
People are already walking along the lane,
and the market is becoming so busy,
that indeed the morning, the pale one,
already raises its white wings.
And I am worried about our neighbors,
lest you give offense;
because they don't know how deeply
I love you and you love me.
So, beloved, go now!
See, the morning breaks.
When the sun in heaven shining
drives from the field the clear pearls,
I must also, weeping, leave the pearl
that was my wealth.
What sparkles like day to the others
seems night to my eyes,
since separation lies like fearful darkness before me
when the dawn awakens.
Go, beloved, go now!
See, the morning breaks.
So flee from my arms!
since if you tarry too long,
for a brief moment of ardor
we may suffer enduring sorrow.
For we still must get through a day
in the pains of Purgatory
while hope in beams far off
shows us heaven's glory.
So, beloved, go now!
See, the morning breaks.

Italian Songbook

1. *Auch kleine Dinge*

Even little things can delight us,
even little things can be precious.
Consider how we love to bedeck ourselves with pearls;
they are costly and are only small.
Consider how small is the olive fruit,
and yet it is sought for its fineness.
Think only of the rose, how small it is,
and yet how lovely it smells, as you know.

2. *Mir ward gesagt*

They told me you are traveling far away.
Ah, where are you going, my beloved life?
I would fain know the day when you depart;
with tears I will accompany you.
With tears I will water your path—
think of me, and hope will shine on me!
With tears I am with you everywhere—
think of me, do not forget, my heart!

3. *Ihr seid die Allerschönste*

You are the most beautiful far and wide,
much lovelier than the abundant flowers in May.
Orvieto's cathedral does not rise up with such splendor,
nor does Viterbo's grandest fountain.
So lofty is your own charm and enchantment,
the cathedral of Siena must bow before you.
Ah, you are so rich in charm and grace,
the cathedral of Siena itself is not your equal.

4. *Gesegnet sei, durch den die Welt entstund*

Blessed be He through whom the world arose;
how excellently He created it in every way!
He created the sea with its infinite depths,
He created the ships that glide over it,
He created Paradise with eternal light,
He created beauty and your countenance.

5. *Selig ihr Blinden*

Blessed ye blind, who cannot see
the charms that kindle our ardor;
blessed ye deaf, who can, without dismay,
ridicule the groans of lovers;
blessed ye mute, who cannot make
your heart's need understood to women;
blessed ye dead, who have been buried!
you shall have peace from love's torments.

6. *Wer rief dich denn?*

Who called you then? Who asked you to come?
Who summoned you, if it's such a burden to you?
Go to the sweetheart you prefer,
go where your thoughts are.
Just go where your feelings and mind are!
I can gladly do without your coming here.
Go to the sweetheart you prefer!
Who called you then? Who asked you to come?

7. *Der Mond hat eine schwere Klag' erhoben*

The moon has raised a serious grievance
and brought the matter before the Lord:
He wants to stay in the heavens no longer,
since you have taken away his splendor.
When he last counted the multitude of stars,
the full number was incomplete;
two of the most beautiful you have stolen:
the two eyes there, which have dazzled me.

8. *Nun lass uns Frieden schliessen*

Now let us make peace, dearest life,
too long we have been feuding.
If you don't want to, I shall surrender to you;
how could we fight to the death?
Kings and princes make peace,
and thus shouldn't lovers crave it?
Princes and soldiers make peace,
and should two lovers then fail?
Do you believe that what such great lords achieve
a pair of contented hearts cannot accomplish?

9. *Dass doch gemalt all' deine Reize wären*

If only all your charms were painted,
and then the heathen prince were to find the portrait,
he would present you with a great offering,
and lay his crown in your hands.
To the true faith would have to be converted
his whole kingdom, to its farthest reaches.
Throughout the land it would be announced
that each should become a Christian and love you.
Every heathen would forthwith convert
and become a good Christian and love you.

10. *Du denkst mit einem Fädchen mich zu fangen*

You think that with a thread you can catch me,
with a mere glance make me fall in love?
I've already caught others who soared higher;
you really mustn't trust me when you see me laugh.
I've already caught others, believe it truly.
I am in love, just not with you.

11. *Wie lange schon war immer mein Verlangen*

How long I have had this desire:
ah, if only a musician would love me!
Now the Lord has granted me my wish
and sends me one, with a pink-and-white complexion.
Here he comes now, with a gentle manner,
and lowers his head, and plays the violin.

12. *Nein, junger Herr*

No, young man, one doesn't do such things, really;
one takes care to behave properly.
For everyday I am good enough, yes?
But you seek something better on holidays.
No, young man, if you thus continue to indulge,
your everyday sweetheart will give notice.

13. *Hoffährtig seid Ihr, schönes Kind*

You are haughty, beautiful child,
and you get on your high horse with your suitors.
If someone speaks to you, you hardly reply,
as if a pleasant greeting cost you too dearly.
You are no daughter of Alexander,
no kingdom will be your dowry,
and if you don't want gold, then take tin;
if you don't want love, take scorn.

14. *Geselle, woll'n wir uns in Kutten hüllen*

Comrade, shall we wrap ourselves in cowls,
leave the world to those it may delight?
Then let us knock on door after door in the quiet:
"Give to a poor monk for Jesus' sake."
O beloved Father, you must come later,
when we have taken the bread out of the oven.
O beloved Father, just come again later,
a daughter of mine lies sick in bed.
—And if she is sick, let me go to her,
lest she perhaps die unshriven.
And if she is sick, let me look after her,
that she may make her confession to me.
Close door and window, that no one will disturb us,
while I hear the confession of the poor child!

15. *Mein Liebster ist so klein*

My sweetheart is so small that without bending
he sweeps my room with his locks.
When he went to the little garden to pick jasmine,
he was terrified by a snail.
Then when he sat down in the house to catch his breath,
a fly drove him out;
and when he stepped up to my little window,
a horsefly stove his head in.
Cursed be all flies, gnats, horseflies—
and whoever has a sweetheart from the Maremma!
Cursed be all flies, gnats, midges—
and whoever, when he kisses, must bend so low!

16. *Ihr jungen Leute*

You young people going to battle,
take care of my beloved.
See that he behaves bravely under fire;
he was never in a war in all his life.
Never let him sleep under the open sky;
he is so delicate, it might have bad consequences.
Don't let him sleep under the moon;
he would die, he isn't used to it.

17. *Und willst du deinen Liebsten sterben sehen*

And if you would see your lover die,
don't wear your hair in curls, darling.
Let it swing free from your shoulders behind;
it looks like threads of pure gold.
Like golden threads, which the wind moves—
beautiful is the hair, beautiful is she who bears it!
Golden threads, silken threads innumerable—
beautiful is the hair, beautiful is she who combs it!

18. *Heb' auf dein blondes Haupt*

Raise your blonde head and do not sleep,
and don't let yourself be lured by slumber.
I'll speak to you four weighty words,

none of which should you ignore.
The first: that my heart breaks for you,
the second: I want to belong only to you,
the third: that I entrust my welfare to you,
the last: my soul loves you alone.

19. *Wir haben Beide lange Zeit geschwiegen*

We have both been silent a long time,
now suddenly speech has returned to us.
The angels that fly down from heaven
have brought peace after the war.
The angels of God have flown down
bringing peace with them.
The angels of love came overnight
and have brought peace to my breast.

20. *Mein Liebster singt am Haus*

My beloved sings at the house in the moonlight,
and I must lie listening here in bed.
I turn away from my mother and weep,
My tears are blood, they do not run dry.
I have wept the broad stream on the bed;
From crying, I don't know whether the morning has dawned.
I wept the broad stream on the bed from longing;
the bloody tears have blinded me.

21. *Man sagt mir, deine Mutter woll' es nicht*

They tell me your mother doesn't approve of it;
so stay away, my darling, do what she desires.
Ah dearest, no! do not do what she wants,
come to me, do it in spite of her, secretly.
No, my beloved, obey her no longer,
do it in spite of her, come more often than before!
No, don't listen to her, no matter what she says;
do it in spite of her, my love, come every day!

22. *Ein Ständchen Euch zu bringen*

To bring you a serenade I've come here,
if it's not inconvenient for the master of the house.
You have a beautiful daughter. It might be good
if you did not guard her so strictly at home.
And if she is already in bed, I beg you,
let her know, for my sake,
that her devoted follower came by,
who keeps her in his thoughts day and night,
and that in the day that counts twenty-four,
I miss her twenty-five hours.

23. *Was für ein Lied soll dir gesungen werden*

What kind of song should be sung to you
that would be worthy of you? Where might I find it?
I'd like most to dig it up from deep in the earth,
sung, until now, by no creature.
A song that neither man nor woman till today
has heard or sung, not even the oldest people.

24. *Ich esse nun mein Brod nicht trocken mehr*

I now eat my bread dry no more,*
a thorn has remained stuck in my foot.
In vain to right and left I look about,
and no one do I find who wants to love me.
If only there were a little old man
who would show me a little love and respect.
I mean in particular a well-proportioned,

respectable old man, of about my age.
I mean, to be perfectly open,
a little old man about fourteen years old.

*That is, it is wet with tears.

25. *Mein Liebster hat zu Tische mich geladen*

My dearest invited me to dine with him
and yet had no house in which to receive me,
neither wood nor hearth for cooking or for roasting;
even the pot had long since broken.
A little cask of wine was also wanting,
and glasses he had none at all in use;
the table was narrow, the tablecloth no better,
the bread stone-hard, and utterly dull the knife.

26. *Ich liess mir sagen und mir ward erzählt*

I was told, and it was related to me,
that handsome Toni is starving himself to death;
since love so exceedingly torments him,
he devours seven loaves for each molar.
After the meal, to toughen his digestion,
he consumes a sausage and seven loaves,
and if Tonina does not relieve his pain,
before long famine and dearth will break out.

27. *Schon streckt' ich aus im Bett*

No sooner had I stretched out my weary limbs in bed
than your image arose before me, you dear one.
Immediately I jump up, put on my shoes again,
and wander through the city with my lute.
I sing and play till the street resounds;
so many a girl hearkens, I am soon gone.
So many girls did my song touch,
while the wind had already carried away song and music.

28. *Du sagst mir, dass ich keine Fürstin sei*

You tell me that I am no princess;
you likewise are not descended from the Spanish throne.
No, my good fellow, you arise at cock's crow,
you go to the field, and not in a state carriage.
You mock me for my lowliness,
but poverty does no injury to noble blood.
You mock me for lacking crown and coat of arms,
and you yourself travel on shanks' mare.

29. *Wohl kenn' ich Eueren Stand*

Of course, I know your rank, which is no small one.
You had no need to stoop so low
to love such a poor and lowly creature,
seeing that the most beautiful women bow before you.
You easily outdid the handsomest men,
that's why I know you're just having fun with me.
You're mocking me, people have tried to warn me;
but, ah, you're so good-looking! Who can be angry with you?

30. *Lass sie nur gehn, die so die Stolze spielt*

Just let her go, who plays the proud one so,
the wonder herb from the field of flowers.
One sees where her shining eye is directed,
since day after day another pleases her.
She carries on just like Tuscany's river,
which every mountain stream must follow.
She carries on like the Arno, it seems to me:
one minute she has many suitors, the next not one.*

*As in the hot summer months the Arno's tributaries leave it to fend
   for itself.

31. *Wie soll ich fröhlich sein*

How should I be gay and even laugh,
when you are always obviously angry with me?
You come only once every hundred years,
and then as if you had been ordered to.
Why do you come if your family doesn't want you to?
Set my heart free, then you may depart.
At home with your people live in peace,
since what heaven desires happens here below.
Keep peace with your people at home,
since what heaven desires does not fail to happen.

32. *Was soll der Zorn, mein Schatz*

What is the anger, my dear, that inflames you?
I'm not aware of any sin I've committed.
Ah, sooner take a well-sharpened knife
and approach me, pierce my breast.
And if a knife won't serve, then take a sword,
that the spring of my blood will spurt toward heaven.
And if a sword won't serve, take a dagger's blade
and wash in my blood all my torment.

33. *Sterb' ich, so hüllt in Blumen meine Glieder*

When I die, cover my limbs in flowers;
I do not wish that you should dig a grave for me.
Opposite those walls lay me down,
where you have so often seen me.
There lay me down in rain or wind;
gladly I die, if it is for you, beloved child.
There lay me down in sunshine and rain;
I die happily if I die for you.

34. *Und steht Ihr früh am Morgen auf*

And when you arise early in the morning from bed,
you sweep away from the heavens all the clouds,
you lure the sun onto the mountains there,
and cherubs appear, competing
to bring you shoes and garments posthaste.
Then when you go out to holy matins,
you draw everyone with you,
and when you approach the blessed place,
you light the lamps with your glance.
You take holy water, make the sign of the cross,
and then moisten your white brow,
and bow and bend your knee as well;
oh, how beautifully everything becomes you!
How fair and blessed has God gifted you,
that you have received the crown of beauty!
How fair and blessed you walk through life;
the palm of beauty was given to you.

35. *Benedeit die sel'ge Mutter*

Blessed the happy mother of whom you were born so lovely,
so elect in beauty—
my longing flies toward you!
You so lovely of gesture,
you the fairest on earth,
you my jewel, my delight, sweet one, blessed are you!
When I from afar languish
and look on
your beauty,
see how I tremble and groan,
so that I can hardly hide it!
And in my breast I feel violent flames rising,
which destroy my peace,
ah, madness seizes me!

36. *Wenn du, mein Liebster, steigst zum Himmel auf*

When you, my dearest, ascend to heaven,
I shall carry my heart to you in my hand.
So lovingly you will embrace me thereupon,
then we shall lay ourselves at the feet of the Lord.
And when the Lord God sees our love's sufferings,
he will make one heart from two loving hearts,
into one heart he will join two together,
in Paradise, bathed in the light of heaven's flames.

37. *Wie viele Zeit verlor ich, dich zu lieben!*

How much time did I lose in loving you!
had I only loved God all that time.
A place in Paradise would be reserved for me,
a saint would then sit at my side.
And because I loved you, beautiful fresh face,
I forfeited the light of Paradise,
and because I loved you, beautiful violet,
I am now unable to enter into Paradise.

38. *Wenn du mich mit den Augen streifst und lachst*

When you glance at me and laugh,
and lower your eyes and incline your chin toward your
    bosom,
I ask that you first make a sign to me,
so that I can also subdue my heart,
that I may subdue my heart, tame and quiet,
when it wants to burst forth with great love,
that I may keep my heart within my breast,
when it wants to burst out with great desire.

39. *Gesegnet sei das Grün*

Blessed be green and whoever wears it!
A green dress will I have made,
A green dress is worn also by the spring meadow.
In green the darling of my eyes clothes himself.
To dress in green is the hunter's custom,
a green suit my beloved also wears;
green is beautifully becoming to all things,
from green grows every beautiful fruit.

40. *O wär' dein Haus durchsichtig wie ein Glas*

Oh, would that your house were transparent like a glass,
my beloved man, when I steal past!
then I would see you inside constantly,
how I would gaze on you with my whole soul!
How many glances my heart would send to you,
more than there are drops in the river in March!
How many glances would I send toward you,
more than the drops that sprinkle down in the rain!

41. *Heut Nacht erhob ich mich um Mitternacht*

Tonight I arose at midnight,
because my heart had furtively stolen away.

I asked: Heart, where are you rushing so furiously?
It spoke: Only to see you had it run away.
Now see how it must be with my love:
my heart escapes my breast so as to see you.

42. *Nicht länger kann ich singen*

No longer can I sing, because the wind
blows hard and makes it hard to breathe.
I fear too that the time trickles away to no avail.
If I were certain, I wouldn't now go to bed.
If I knew something, I wouldn't walk home
and lose this beautiful time alone.

43. *Schweig' einmal still*

Shut up for once, you horrible windbag there!
Your accursed singing disgusts me.
And if you carried on that way till tomorrow morning,
you'd still not come up with one decent song.
Shut up for once and hit the hay!
The serenade of a donkey I'd prefer!

44. *O wüsstest du, wie viel ich deinetwegen*

Oh, if you knew how much, on your account,
false renegade, I've suffered at night,
while you lay in your locked house
and I passed the time outside.
For rosewater the rain served me,
the lightning brought me tidings of love;
I played dice with the storm,
as under your eaves I kept watch.
My bed was made under your eaves,
the sky lay spread like a blanket above,
the threshold of your door, that was my pillow,
poor me, ah, what I've had to endure!

45. *Verschling' der Abgrund meines Liebsten Hütte*

May the abyss swallow up my beloved's cottage,
in its place may a lake bubble up directly.
May the heavens above shower down lead bullets,
and a snake make its home there.
May a snake of a poisonous kind house in it,
which will poison him who was untrue to me.
In it may a snake house, swollen with poison,
and bring death to him who decided to betray me!

46. *Ich hab' in Penna einen Liebsten wohnen*

I have a boyfriend who lives in Penna,
in the Maremma plains yet another,
one in the lovely harbor of Ancona,
for the fourth I must travel to Viterbo;
another lives yonder in Casentino,
the next lives in the same town with me,
and yet another have I in Magione,
four in La Fratta, ten in Castiglione.

Glossary of German Terms

allmählig, gradually
ängstlich, anxiously
anmuthig, graceful(ly)
anschwellend, swelling, crescendo
aufflammend, flaring up
aus, from
Ausdruck, expression
ausdrucksvoll, expressively
äusserst, extremely

bedeutend, significantly
belebter, more animated
beschleunigend, quickening
bestimmt, firm
bewegt, animated, *bewegter*, more
   animated
Bewegung, motion
breit, broad, *breiter*, broader

das, the
doch, but
drängend, pressing, stringendo
durchweg, throughout

eilen, hurry
ein, a
Empfindung, feeling
ersterbend, dying away
erstes, first, *erstes Zeitmaass*, tempo
   primo
etwas, somewhat

fast, always
Ferne, distance
feurig, fiery
fliessend, flowing
flüsternd, whispering
frei, freely
frisch, lively, brisk

gedämpft, damped
gedehnt, drawn out
gefühlvoll, tenderly, expressively
gehalten, restrained
gemächlich, comfortably
gemessen, measured
gesteigert, louder

gesteigertem, increasing
getragen, solemn(ly)
Grazie, grace

Harmonienwechsel, change of harmony
Hauptzeitmaass, tempo primo
heftig, vigorously, violently
herzlich, heartfelt
hingebend, submitting, yielding
höhnisch, scornfully
Humor, humor

I., 1st
im, in the
immer, always, constantly
in, in, to
innig, fervently, heartfelt

ja, absolutely
jedem, every
jedoch, nevertheless

kläglich, dolefully
kokett, flirtatiously
kurz, short

lachend, laughing
langsam, slow, *langsamer*, slow, slower
lebhaft, lively, briskly, *lebhafter*, livelier
leicht, light(ly)
leidenschaftlich, passionately, *leiden-*
   schaftlichstem, most passionate
leise, softly, delicately

majestätisch, majestically
Marschtempo, march tempo
mässig(em), moderato, moderate(ly)
mit, with
munter, gaily

nach, after
nachlassend, subsiding, decrescendo
nicht, not, do not

ohne, without

Pedal, pedal

rasch, impetuously, quickly
recht, quite, very
ruhig(e), peaceful, *ruhiger*, more peace-
   fully

sanfte, gentle, gently
schleppend, dragging
schmerzlich, painfully
schnell, fast
schwankend, unsteadily
schwer, heavy
sehr, very

tiefer, deep
Triller, trill

übergehend, changing
und, and
unhörbar, inaudible
unruhig, restless

verklingend, dying away
Verschiebung, una corda
Viertelbewegung, quarter-note motion
voriges, preceding
vorzutragen, to be played

Wärme, warmth
weich, mildly, supplely
weiter, far
wenig, little
wie, as though
wieder, again
wild, unrestrained

zaghaft, with trepidation, hesitating
zart, gentle, gently
Zeitmass, Zeitmaass, tempo
ziemlich, somewhat, rather
zögernd, hesitating
zunehmend, increasing, accelerating
Zurückhalten, restraint
zurückhalten, zurückhaltend, zurück-
   halt., held back, *zurückhaltender*,
   more restrained

SPANISH SONGBOOK
SPANISCHES LIEDERBUCH

SPIRITUAL SONGS
GEISTLICHE LIEDER

1. Nun bin ich dein

le_sen, zu dir steht all mein Hof_fen, mein in_nerst We_sen ist al_le_zeit dir of_fen.

Komm, mich zu lö_sen vom Fluch des Bö_

_sen, der mich so hart __ be_trof_fen! Du Stern der See, du Port der Won_

_nen, von der im Weh die Wun_den Heil ge_won _ _ _ _ _nen,

heilt al_len Harm und Scha_den.

Ich lei_ _de schwer und

wohl ver_dien_te Stra_fen.

Mir bangt so sehr, bald To_

_des_schlaf zu schla_fen.

Tritt du ein_her, und durch das

Meer o füh_ _re mich zum Ha_ _fen.

2. Die du Gott gebarst, du Reine

Langsam und sehr innig.

Die du Gott ge - barst, ____ du Rei - ne,

und al - lei - ne uns ge - löst aus un - sern Ket - ten, mach mich

fröh - lich, der ich wei - ne, denn nur dei - ne Huld und

Gna_de mag uns ret_ten. Her_ _ _rin, ganz _ _ zu dir mich

wen_de, dass sich en_de die_se Qual und die_ses Grau_en,

dass der Tod mich furcht _ _ los fän_ de, und nicht

blen_de mich das Licht der Him_mels_au_en.

Weil du un _ be _ fleckt ge _ bo _ ren, aus _ er _ ko _ _ _ ren zu des

molto cresc._ _

ew'_ gen Ruh_mes Stät _ ten — wie mich Lei _ den auch _ um_

f *sf* *p* *sf*

flo _ ren, un _ _ ver _ lo_ren bin ich doch, willst du mich ret _ _ _

p *f* *ff* *mf* *p*

ten.

p *dimin._ _ _* *pp*

3. Nun wandre, Maria

(St. Joseph sings:)

Langsam und ruhig.

Nun wan - dre, Ma - ri - a, nun wan - dre nur fort. Schon krä - hen die Häh - ne und nah ist der Ort. Nun wan - dre, Ge - lieb - te, du Klein - od mein, und bal - de wir wer - den in Beth - le - hem sein.

9

nah ist der Ort. ____ Wär erst be_stan _ den dein Stünd_lein, Ma_rie, die

gu _ te Bot _ schaft gut lohnt' ich sie. Das E _ se_lein hie

gäb' ich drum fort! Schon krä _ hen die Häh _ ne, komm!

nah ist der Ort. ____

4. Die ihr schwebet um diese Palmen

Die ihr schwe __ bet um die _ se Pal _ _ _ men in Nacht und Wind, ihr heil' _ gen En _ gel, stil _ let die Wi _ pfel! es schlum _ mert mein Kind.

Ihr Pal - men
von Beth - le - hem im Win - des - brau - - - sen,
wie mögt ihr heu - te so zor - - nig sau - sen!
O rauscht nicht al - so!

schwei _ _ get, nei _ get euch leis' und lind; _____

stil _ let die Wi _ pfel! es schlum _ mert mein

Kind. _____

Der Him _ _ mels _ kna _ be dul _ det Be _

schwer _ de, ach, wie so müd' er ward vom Leid der

Er _ de. Ach nun im Schlaf ihn lei _ se ge_

sänf _ tigt die Qual zer _ rinnt, stil _ let ihr Wi _ pfel!

es schlum _ mert mein Kind.

Grim-mi-ge Käl-te sau-set her-nie-der, wo-mit nur deck' ich des Kind-leins Glie-der! O all ihr En-gel, die ihr ge-flü——gelt wan-delt im Wind, stil-let die

5. Führ mich, Kind, nach Bethlehem

Ziemlich langsam.

Führ mich, Kind, nach Beth_le_hem! dich, mein

Gott, dich will ich sehn. Wem ge_läng' es, wem, oh_ne dich zu

dir zu gehn! Rütt_le mich, dass ich er_wa_che, ru_fe mich,

so will ich schrei_ten; gieb die Hand mir, mich zu lei _ ten, dass ich auf den Weg_

_ _ _ mich ma _ che. Dass ich schau_e Beth _ le_hem, dor_ten

mei _ nen Gott zu sehn. Wem ge_läng' es, wem, oh _ ne dich zu

dir zu gehn! Von der Sün_de schwe _ rem Kran _ ken bin ich

träg und dumpf be_klom_men. Willst du nicht zu Hül_fe kom_men,

muss ich strau_cheln, muss ich schwanken. Lei_te mich nach Beth_le_

hem, dich, mein Gott, dich will ich sehn. Wem ge_läng' es, wem,

oh_ne dich zu dir zu gehn!

6. Ach, des Knaben Augen

Sanfte Bewegung.

Ach, des Kna _ ben Au _ gen sind mir so schön und klar er-

schie _ nen, und ein Et _ was strahlt aus ih _ nen, das mein gan _ zes Herz ge-

winnt. *(innig.)* Blickt' er doch mit die _ sen sü _ ssen Au _ gen nach den

mei _ nen hin! säh' er dann sein Bild da _ rin, _____ würd' er wohl mich

lie _ bend grü _ ssen. Und so geb' _ ich ganz mich hin,

sei _ nen Au _ gen _ nur zu die _ nen, denn ein Et _ was strahlt aus ih _ _ nen,

das mein gan _ zes Herz ge _ winnt.

7. Mühvoll komm ich und beladen

Sehr langsam und getragen.

Müh _ voll komm' ich und be _ la _ _ den, nimm mich an _ du Hort der Gna _ den! Sieh, ich komm' in Thrä _ nen heiss mit de _ _ mü _ thi ger Ge _ ber _ de, dun _ kel ganz vom Staub der Er _ de.

Du nur schaffest, dass ich weiss _ wie das Vliess der Lämmer wer _ de. Til _ gen

willst du ja den Scha _ den dem, der reu _ ig dich _ um _ fasst; nimm denn,

Herr, von mir die Last. _ müh _ voll komm'ich und be _ la _ _ den.

Lass mich fleh _ end vor dir knie'n.

dass ich ü_ber dei _ ne Füsse Nar _ den Duft und Thrä _ nen gie _ sse, gleich dem

Weib, dem du ver_zieh'n, bis die Schuld wie Rauch zer_fliesse. Der den Schä_cher du ge_la_

_den: „Heu_te noch in E_dens Bann wirst du sein!"

(hingebend.)

O nimm mich an, nimm mich an, du Hort_der Gna_

_ _ _den!

8. Ach, wie lang die Seele schlummert!

Sehr getragen und schwer.

Ach, wie lang die See_le schlum_mert!

Zeit ist's,dass sie sich er_

mun_tre.

Dass man todt sie wäh _ nen dürf_te, al _ so

schläft sie schwer und bang,___ seit sie je _ ner Rausch be _ zwang ___ den in Sün _ dengift sie

schlürfte. Doch nun ih _ rer Sehn _ sucht Licht blendend ihr in's Au _ ge bricht:

Zeit ist's, dass sie sich er-mun-tre. Moch-te sie gleich

taub er-schei-nen bei der En-gel sü-ssem Chor: lauscht sie doch wohl zag empor,

hört sie Gott als Kind-lein wei-nen. Da nach langer Schlummernacht solch ein Tag der

Gnad' ihr lacht, Zeit ist's, dass sie sich er-mun-tre.

9. Herr, was trägt der Boden hier

Sehr langsam und innig.

sol_che Bä_che rin_nen, wird ein Gar_ten da ge_deihn? „Ja, und wis_se!

Krän_ze_lein, gar ver_schied_ne, flicht man drin_nen: O mein

Herr, zu wes_sen Zier win_det man die Krän_ze? sprich! „Die von Dor_nen

sind für mich, die von Blu_men reich' ich dir.“

10. Wunden trägst du mein Geliebter

Langsam und mit tiefer Empfindung.

so zu fär _ ben dei _ ne Stirn mit Blut und Schweiss? „Die _ se Ma _ _ le

sind der Preis, dich, o See _ le, zu er _ wer _ ben. An den Wun _ den

muss ich ster _ ben, weil ich dich ge _ liebt so heiss.“ Könnt' ich, Herr, für

dich sie tra _ gen, da es To _ des _ wun _ den sind. „Wenn dies Leid _ dich

Erstes Zeitmaass.

— recht zu min _ nen, der da stirbt vor Lie _ _ besgluth."

Wun _ den trägst du __ mein Ge_lieb _ ter, und sie schmer_zen

dich; trüg' ich sie statt dei _ ner, ich!

WORLDLY SONGS
WELTLICHE LIEDER

1. Klinge, klinge, mein Pandero

Wenn du, mun _ tres Ding, ver _ stän _ dest mei _ ne Qual _____ und sie em _

pfän _ dest, je _ der Ton, den du ent _ sen _ dest, wür _ de kla _

_ gen mei _ nen Schmerz.

Bei des Tan-zes Drehn und Nei-gen schlag' ich wild ____ den Takt zum

Rei-gen, dass nur die Ge-dan-ken schwei-gen, die mich

mah-nen an den Schmerz. ____

Ach, ihr Herrn, dann will im Schwingen oft _ _ mals mir die Brust zer _

sprin - gen; und zum Angstschrei wird mein Sin - gen, denn an an _ _ dres denkt mein

Herz. _____

2. In dem Schatten meiner Locken

Doch um_sonst ist meine Mü - he, weil die Win _ _ de sie zer_sau _ sen.

Locken_schat _ ten, Windes_sau _ sen schläferten den Liebsten ein.

Weck' ich ihn nun auf? — Ach nein!

Hö_ren muss ich, wie ihn grä _ me, dass er schmach _ tet schon so lan _ ge, dass ihm

3. Seltsam ist Juanas Weise

Mässig.

Selt‿sam ist Ju‿a‿nas Wei‿se. Wenn ich steh' in Trau‿

‿rigkeit, wenn ich seufz' und sa‿ge: heut, „mor‿‿‿gen" spricht sie lei‿se.

Trüb' ist sie, wenn ich mich freu‿e; lu‿stig singt sie, wenn ich

weiss sie stets den Blick zu sen_ken, um ihn gleich em_por zu len_ken,

schlag' ich auch den mei_nen nie _ der. Wenn ich sie als Heil'_ge prei _ se,

nennt sie Dä_mon mich im Streit, _ wenn ich seufz' und sa_ge: heut, „mor_

_ gen" spricht sie lei _ _ se. Sieg_los heiss' ich auf der

Stel _ le,   rühm' ich mei _ nen Sieg be _ schei _ den;   hoff' ich auf des Himmels

Freu _ den,   pro _ phe _ zeit sie mir die Höl _ le.   Ja, so ist ihr Herz von

Ei _ se,   säh' sie ster _ ben mich vor Leid,   hör _ te mich noch seufzen:

heut,   „mor _ _ _ gen" spräch' sie lei _ se.

4. Treibe nur mit Lieben Spott

Sehr mässig.

Trei‐be nur mit Lie‐ben Spott, Ge‐lieb‐te mein;

spot‐tet doch der Lie‐bes‐gott der‐einst auch dein! Magst an Spotten nach Ge‐fal‐len du dich wei‐den;

etwas bewegter.

von dem Wei‐be kommt uns Al‐len Lust und Lei‐‐den.

Erstes Zeitmaass.

Trei‐be nur mit Lie‐ben Spott, Ge‐lieb‐te mein;

spot‐tet doch der Lie‐bes‐gott der‐einst auch dein! Bist auch jetzt zu stolz zum

poco rit.

etwas bewegter.

Erstes Zeitmaass.

Minnen, glaub', o glau-be: Lie-be wird dich doch ge - win-nen sich zum Rau-be, wenn du spot-test mei-ner

etwas bewegter.

Noth, Ge-lieb-te mein; spot-tet doch der Liebes-gott der-einst auch dein! Wer da lebt in Fleisch, er-

wä-ge al-le Stunden: Amor schläft und plötz-lich re-ge schlägt er Wun - - den.

Erstes Zeitmaass.

Treibe nur mit Lie-ben Spott, Ge-lieb-te mein; spot-tet doch der Liebesgott der-einst auch dein!

poco rit.

5. Auf dem grünen Balcon

Im _ mer nach dem Brauch der Mäd _ chen träuft ins Glück ein

bis _ chen Pein: _____ Mit den Au _ gen blin _ zelt sie freund _ lich,

mit dem Fin _ ger sagt ____ sie mir: Nein!

Wie sich nur in ihr ver _ tra _ gen

hin so fein, _____ mit den Au - gen blinzelt sie

freund - lich, mit dem Fin - ger sagt _____ sie mir:

Nein! _____

6. Wenn du zu den Blumen gehst

Anmuthig fliessend, in sehr mässigem Tempo.

Wenn du zu den Blu_men gehst, pflü_cke die schön_sten, dich zu schmücken.

Ach, wenn du in dem Gärt_lein stehst, müss__test du dich sel__ber pflücken.

Al____le Blu_men wis_sen ja, dass du hold bist__ oh_ne glei_chen.

Und die Blu _ me, _ die dich sah _ Farb' und Schmuck muss ihr er_

blei _ _ _ chen. Wenn du zu den Blu _ men gehst,

pflü _ cke die schön_sten, dich zu schmü_cken. Ach, wenn du in dem Gärt_lein stehst, müss _

_ test du dich sel _ _ ber pflü_cken. Lieb _ _ li_cher als Ro_sen

53

7. Wer sein holdes Lieb verloren

Sehr mässig.

Wer sein hol_des Lieb ver _ lo_ren, weil er Lie _ be nicht ver_steht, bes_ser wär' er nie ge _ bo_ren.

Ich ver_lor sie dort im Gar_ten, da sie Ro _ sen brach und Blü_then.

Hell auf ih_ren Wan_gen glüh_ten Scham und Lust _____ in hol_ _der Zier. Und von

poco rit. *a tempo.* *a tempo.*

Lie_be sprach sie mir; doch ich gröss_ter al_ler Tho_ren wusste

kei_ne Ant_wort ihr_ wär' ich nimmer_mehr ge_bo_ren. Ich ver_

lor sie dort im Gar_ten, da sie sprach von Lie_bes_pla_gen, denn ich wag_te nicht zu sa_gen, wie ich

ganz ihr ei_gen bin. In die Blu_men sank sie hin;

doch ich gröss_ter al_ler Tho_ren zog auch da_von nicht Ge_winn,__ wär' ich

nim_mer_mehr ge_bo_ren! Wer sein hol_des Lieb ver_lo_ren, weil er

Lie_be nicht ver_steht, bes_ser wär' er nie ge_bo_ren.

8. Ich fuhr über Meer

Nach Glück __ ich jag-te, an Lei __ den krankt' ich; als

immer zurückhaltender.   langsam.

Recht ____ ver - langt' ___ ich was Lie __ be ver-sag - te.

a tempo.   poco rit.

Ich hofft' und wag __ - te __ kein Glück ___ mir ge-dieh,

langsam.   Erstes Zeitmaass.

und   so schaut' ich es   nie.

Trug oh_ne Kla_ _ ge die Lei_den, die bö_sen, und

immer zurückhaltender. langsam.

dacht', es lö_ _ _sen sich ab _ die Ta_ge.

a tempo. poco rit. langsam.

die fröh_ _ _li_chen Ta_ge, wie ei_len sie! _ ich _ er_eil_te sie

Erstes Zeitmaass.

immer ein wenig langsamer

nie! _ _ _

9. Blindes Schauen, dunkle Leuchte

Gemessen, doch leidenschaftlich.

Blin _ des Schau _ en, dun _ kle Leuch _ te, Ruhm voll Weh, er _ storb' _ nes Le _ ben, Un _ heil, das ein

Heil mir däuch _ te, freud' _ ges Wei _ nen, Lust voll Be _ ben, sü _ sse Gal _ le.

10. Eide, so die Liebe schwur

Sehr gehalten.

Ei — de, so die Lie — be schwur, schwa — che Bürgen sind sie nur. Sitzt die Lie — be zu Ge — richt, dann, Se — ñor, ver — ges — set nicht, dass sie nie nach Recht und Pflicht, im — mer nur nach Gunst ver — fuhr.

leich_ten Händlein schwan_ken, schreibt euch keiner nach der Schnur. Ei_de, so die

Lie_be schwur, schwa_che Bürgen sind sie nur. Sind die Bürgen ge_gen_wär_tig,

ein wenig zurückhalt.

al_le samt des Spruch's ge_wär_tig, ma_chen sie das Ur_theil fer_tig;— vom Vollziehen kei_ne

a tempo.
zurückhaltend.

Spur! Ei_de, so die Lie_be schwur, schwa_che Bürgen sind sie nur.

11. Herz verzage nicht geschwind

nen _ nen und wie Feu _ er _ fun _ _ ken bren _ nen. Drum ver _ _

bedeutend langsamer. *rit.* **Erstes Zeitmaass.**

za _ ge nicht ge _ schwind, weil die Wei _ ber Wei _ ber sind. Lass ____ dir nicht den Sinn ver _

wir _ ren, wenn ____ sie sü _ sse Wei _ sen gir _ ren; möch _ _ ten dich mit Lis _ ten

langsam und gedehnt. **Erstes Zeitmaass.**

kir _ ren, ma _ _ chen dich mit Ränken blind; weil die Wei _ ber Wei _ ber sind.

12. Sagt, seid Ihr es, feiner Herr

Sehr lebhaft und mit Grazie.

Sagt, seid Ihr es, feiner Herr, der da jüngst so hübsch gesprungen und ge_sprungen und ge_sun_gen? Seid Ihr der, ___ vor dessen Keh_le Kei_ _ner mehr zu Wort ge_kom_men? habt die Ba_cken voll ge_nom_men, sangt gar

(kokett.)

immer staccato.

✳) Der bequemern Spielart wegen können die in Klammern gesetzten Noten in der Klavierbegleitung auch weggelassen werden.

*) For the sake of easier performance, the notes in parentheses in the piano accompaniment can even be omitted.

ar _ tig, oh _ ne Feh _ le. Ja, Ihr seid's, bei meiner See _ le,

der so mit uns um _ gesprungen und ge _ sprungen und ge _ sun _ gen.

Seid Ihr's, der ___ auf Cas _ tag _ net _ ten und Ge _ sang sich nie ___ ver _ stand, der die

Lie _ be nie ge _ kannt, der da floh vor Wei _ ber _ ket _ ten?

poco *rit.*　　　　　a tempo.

Ja, Ihr seid's; doch möcht ich wet _ ten, manch ein Lieb habt Ihr um _ schlun _ gen

und ge _ sprun _ gen und ge _ sun _ gen.

Seid Ihr der, der Tanz und Lie _ der so her _ aus _ strich oh _ _ ne

Mass? _____ Seid Ihr's, _ der _____ im Win _ _ kel

sass und nicht reg _ te sei _ ne Glie _ der?

Ja Ihr seid's, ich kenn' Euch wie _ der, der zum Gäh _ nen

uns ge _ zwun _ gen und ge _ sprun _ gen und ge _ sun _ _ _

_ _ _ _ gen!

13. Mögen alle bösen Zungen

Schlim _ me, schlimme Re_den flüs_tern eu _ _ _ re Zun_gen scho _ nungs_los, doch _

etwas zurückhaltend.　　　　　　　　　　　　　　　　　　　　a tempo.

_ ich weiss es, sie sind lüs_tern nach un _ _ schuld'_gem Blu_te bloss.

Nim_mer soll es mich be_küm_mern, schwatzt _ so viel es euch be_liebt;

wer mich liebt, den lieb' ich wie_der, und ich lieb' _____ und bin ge _ liebt.

14. Köpfchen, Köpfchen, nicht gewimmert
(Preciosa's charm against headaches)

Köpf-chen, Köpf-chen, nicht ge-wim-mert, halt dich wa-cker,

halt dich mun-ter, stütz' zwei gu-te Säul-chen un-ter, heil _ sam aus Ge-duld ge-

zim-mert! Hoff _ nung schim-mert, wie sich's auch ver-

schlim_mert und dich kümmert. Musst mit Grä_men dir nichts zu Her_zen

neh_men, ja kein Mär_chen, dass zu Berg dir stehn die Här_chen; da sei

Gott da_vor und der Rie_se Chri_sto_phor! da sei Gott da_vor und der Rie_se Chri_sto_

phor!

15. Sagt ihm, dass er zu mir komme

Mässig, innig und leidenschaftlich.

Sagt ihm, dass er zu mir kom _ me, denn je mehr sie mich drum schel _ ten, ach je mehr wächst mei _ ne Glut! O zum Wanken bringt die Lie _ be nichts auf Er _ _ den; durch ihr Zan _ ken wird sie nur ge _ dop _ _ pelt wer _ den. Sie ge _ fähr _ den mag nicht ih _ rer Nei _ der Wuth; denn je mehr sie

Meine Peiniger sa‿gen oft, ich soll dich las‿‿sen, doch nur ei‿niger wolln wir

uns ins Her‿‿ze fas‿‿sen. Muss ich drum er‿blas‿sen, Tod um Lie‿

(ersterbend.) *(aufflammend.)*

‿‿be lieb‿‿lich thut, und je mehr sie mich drum schel‿ten, ach, je

mehr wächst mei‿ne Glut!

16. Bitt' ihn, o Mutter, bitte den Knaben

Sehr unruhig und leidenschaftlich.

Bitt' ihn, o Mut _ ter, bit _ te den Kna _ ben,

zurückhaltend. a tempo.

nicht mehr zu zie _ len, weil er mich töd _ _ _ tet.

Mut _ ter, o Mut _ ter, die

poco rit. a tempo.

lau _ ni_sche Lie _ be höhnt und versöhnt mich, flieht mich und zieht mich.

17. Liebe mir im Busen zündet einen Brand

gros _ _ _ _ _ _ se Gluth sind zu arm _____ die Mee _ _ _

f   p   cresc. _ _ _   f

_ _ re.   Weil es wohl _____ mir thut wein' __

ff   p   cresc. _ _

_____ ich un _ _ ver _ wandt; _____   Was _

f   ff

_ ser, lie _ be Mut _ ter, eh das Herz _____ ver _ brannt!

sf

18. Schmerzliche Wonnen und wonnige Schmerzen

89

Seel - chen, ge - quäl - tes, in ängst - li - chem Wo - gen fühlst du dich hier hin und

dort hin ge - zo - gen, auf - wärts und ab - wärts. In sol - ches Ge - trie - be

stürzt zwi - schen Him - mel und Höll' uns die Lie - - - - - - be.

Müt - ter - chen, ach, und mit sie - ben - zehn Jah - ren hab ich dies

Han _ gen und Ban _ gen er _ fah _ _ _ ren, Hab's dann ver _ schwo _ ren mit

Thrä _ nen der Reu _ _ _ e; ach, und schon lieb' ich, schon lieb' ich auf's neu _ _

_ _ _ _ e.

immer ff

19. Trau nicht der Liebe

Wo schweifst du nur hin? Lass Rath dir er_thei_len: Das Kind mit den Pfei_len hat Possen im Sinn Die Ta_ _ge, die ei _ len und Lie _ be, gieb Acht! Sie macht dich noch wei _ nen, wo heut du ge_lacht.

Nicht im _ mer ist's hel _ le, nicht im _ mer ist's dun_kel, der

mf *p* *più p*

zunehmend.

Freu _ de Ge _ fun _ kel er _ bleicht __ so schnel_le. Ein fal_scher Ge _ sel _ le ist

mf *p* *f*

etwas zurückhaltend

A _ mor, gieb Acht! Er macht dich noch wei _ nen, wo heut du ge _ lacht. __

più f *ff* *p*

a tempo.

beschleunigend.

dim. *pp* *cresc.* *f*

20. Ach im Maien war's

Leicht bewegt, zart.

Ach im Mai -

en war's, im Mai - en wo die war -

- men Lüf - - te weh - - - en, wo ver - lieb -

- - te Leu - - te pfle - gen ih - ren Lieb -

ich weiss ___ nicht, wann ___ es nach _ _ tet.

a tempo.

poco rit.

dim. - - - - ppp pp

Nur an ei _ _ _

nem Vög _ _ _ lein merkt' ___ ich's, das da drauss ___

cresc. -

___ im Mai _ _ _ en sang; _____ das hat mir

f

ein Schütz _____ ge-töd - tet __ geb' __ ihm Gott den

schlimm - - -sten Dank!

21. Alle gingen, Herz, zur Ruh

22. Dereinst, dereinst Gedanke mein

Langsam.

Der_einst, der_einst Ge_dan_ke mein wirst ru_hig sein._____ Lässt Lie_bes_glut dich still___ nicht wer_den: in küh_ler Er_den da schläfst du gut;

23. Tief im Herzen trag' ich Pein

Langsam und sehr ausdrucksvoll.

Tief im Her — zen trag' ich Pein,

muss nach aus — — sen stil — le sein. Den ge-

lieb — — ten Schmerz ver — heh — le tief — ich vor der Welt Ge-

(sehr zart.)

sicht; und es fühlt ihn nur die See_ le, denn der

Leib ver_dient ihn nicht. Wie der Fun_ ke frei und licht sich ver_

birgt im Kie_ sel_ stein, trag'____ ich____ in_nen

_ tief___ die Pein.

24. Komm, o Tod, von Nacht umgeben

Langsam, mit tiefer Empfindung.

Komm, o Tod, von Nacht um-ge-ben, lei-se komm zu mir ge-gan-gen, dass die Lust, dich zu um-fan-gen, nicht zu-rück mich ruf' ins Le-ben. Komm, so

etwas belebter.

wie der Blitz uns rüh _ ret, den der Don _ ner _

_ nicht ver _ kün _ det, bis er plötz _ _ lich sich ent _

zün _ det und den Schlag ge _ dop _ pelt füh _ ret.

Erstes Zeitmaass.

Al _ so seist du _ mir ge _ ge _ ben, plötz _ lich

stil - lend __ mein Ver - lan - gen, __ dass die Lust, dich __

poco cre - scen - do -

__ zu um - fan - gen, __ nicht zu - rück mich __ ruf' ins

f *p* *pp*

Le - - - - ben.

(zart, doch ausdrucksvoll.)

p

dim.

pp *ppp* *rit.*

25. Ob auch finstre Blicke glitten

Mässig langsam.

Ob auch fin_stre Bli_cke glit_ten, schö_ner Au_gen_stern, aus dir, wird mir doch nicht ab_ge_strit_ten, dass du hast ge_blickt nach mir.____

Wie sich auch der Strahl be_müh_te,

zu ver_wun_den mei_ne Brust, gieht's ein Lei_den, das die Lust, dich___ zu schaun, nicht

reich ver_gü_te? Und so tödt_lich mein Ge_mü_the un_ter

dei_nem Zorn ge_lit_ten, wird mir doch nicht ab_ge_strit_ten, dass du hast ge_blickt nach

mir.___

26. Bedeckt mich mit Blumen

füh - re, be - deckt _____ mich! Ist ja

al - les doch das - sel - be, Lie _____ bes - o - dem o - der Düf -

- - - te von Blu - men. Von Jas - min und weis - sen

Lil - ien sollt ihr ___ hier mein Grab be - rei - ten, ich ster -

ein wenig bewegter

be. Und be - fragt ihr mich: Wo - ran?

zurückhaltend   **Erstes Zeitmaass.**

sag' ich: Un - ter sü - ssen Qua - - - - - len vor

Lie - - - - be - vor Lie - be.

27. Und schläfst du, mein Mädchen

Bewegt.

Und schläfst __ du, mein Mäd _ chen, auf, öft_ne du mir; denn die Stund ist ge_kom_men, da wir wan _ dern von hier. Und bist __ oh_ne Soh_ _ len, leg' kei_ne dir an; durch reis _ sen_de Was _ ser

geht un_se_re Bahn. _____ Durch die tief tie_fen

Was_ser des Qua_dal___qui_vir; denn die Stund' ist ge_kom_men, da wir

wan_dern von hier _____ da wir wan_____dern von

hier. _____

28. Sie blasen zum Abmarsch

Im Marschtempo.

Sie bla_sen zum Ab_marsch, lieb Müt_ter _ lein.

Mein Liebster muss scheiden und lässt mich al _ lein!

Am Himmel die Sterne sind kaum noch geflohn, da feu_ert von fer_ne das Fussvolk schon.

Kaum hört er den Ton, sein Rän _ ze_lein schnürt er, von hin _ nen mar_schiert er,

sehr zurückhaltend.

mein Herz hinter drein. Mein Lieb _ ster muss schei_den und lässt mich al _

a tempo.

etwas langsamer.

lein! Mir ist wie dem Tag, dem die Son _ ne ge_schwunden,mein

noch etwas langsamer.

Trau_ern nicht mag so bal _ de ge_sun_den. Nach nichts ich frag', kei_ne Lust mehr heg'ich, nur

Zwie_sprach pfleg' ich mit mei_ner Pein.

pp

ppp

rit.

Mein Lieb _ ster muss schei_den und lässt _____ mich al _

Erstes Zeitmaass.

p cresc. p cresc. p mf p

a tempo.

lein! _____

pp *pp* *p* *pp*

(allmählig verklingend.)

pppp

29. Weint nicht, ihr Äuglein

Lebhaft.

zurückhaltend

lebhaft:

Weint nicht, ihr Äug-lein!

immer sehr zurückhaltend.

pp

Erstes

wie kann so trü-be wei-nen vor Ei-fer-sucht, wer töd---tet durch Lie-be?

Zeitmaass.

belebt.

Wer selbst Tod bringt.

30. Wer that deinem Füsslein weh?

Sag' Euch mit Auf_rich_tig_keit meine Krank_heit,

meine Wun_de: in den Gar_ten ging ich heut, wo die schönste Nel_ke

stun_de; hat ein Span mich dort verletzt

la_Ma_rio_ne_ta, blu_tet fort und fort bis jetzt ___ la Ma_ri_on. ___

bedeutend langsamer.

„Schö_ne Da_me, wenn Ihr wollt, bin ein Wundarzt gu_ter

zurückhaltend *pp* *noch mehr gedehnt* Erstes Zeitmaass.

Wei_se, will die Wund' Euch stillen lei_se, dass Ihr's kaum ge_wah_ren sollt. Bald sollt Ihr ge-

ne_sen sein la Ma_rio_ne_ta, bald ge_heilt von al_ler Pein,___ la Ma_ri_

on ____ la Ma_ri_on ____ la Ma_ri_on."

31. Deine Mutter, süsses Kind

Bewegt.

Dei_ne Mut_ter, süsses Kind, da sie in __ den

Weh'n ge_le __ gen, brau __ sen hör_te sie den Wind. __

Und so hat sie __ dich ge_bo __ ren mit dem fal _ schen

wind'gen Sinn. Hast du heut ein Herz er_ko _ ren, wirfst es mor_gen treu_los

hin. Doch den zähl' ich __ zu den Tho __ ren, der dich schmäht der

Un __ treu we __ gen: Dein Ge-schick war __ dir ent-ge __ gen;

denn die Mut __ ter, süsses Kind, da sie in __ den Weh'n ge-le __ gen,

brau __ __ sen hör-te sie __ den Wind. __

32. Da nur Leid und Leidenschaft

Soll ich sa _ gen, wie ich's schätze, sind drei Batzen nicht zu viel. Nimmer war's des

Win_des Spiel, ei _ gen _ sin _ nig blieb's _____ im Netz_e.

Aber weil mich drängt die Noth biet' ich nun mein Herz zu

Kauf, schlag' es los zum Meist_ge_bot___ sagt, hat einer Lust da_rauf?

Täg_lich kränkt es mich im Stil _ len und er_freut mich nim_mer_

mehr. Nun wer bie_tet? wer giebt mehr? Fort mit ihm und seinen Grillen! dass sie schlim sind, leuchtet

ein, biet' ich doch mein Herz zu Kauf. Wär es froh, be _ _hielt' _____ ich's

fein ___ sagt, hat ei_ner Lust da_rauf? ___

Kauft ihr's, leb' ich oh _ ne Grä _ _ men   Mag es ha _ ben, wem's be _

liebt!   Nun wer kauft? wer will es neh _ men? Sag' ein Je _ der, was er giebt.

Noch einmal vorm Hammerschlag biet' ich jetzt mein Herz zu Kauf,   dass man   sich entscheiden mag — sagt,

gehalten.   **Erstes Zeitmaass.**

_ hat ei _ ner Lust da _ rauf? _

33. Wehe der, die mir verstrickte

34. Geh, Geliebter, geh jetzt!

Nacht, da die Tren _ _ nung bang mir dun _ kelt,

wenn das Morgenroth er _ _ wacht. _____ Geh, ___ Ge_lieb_ter,

lebhaft drängend und beschleunigend.

geh jetzt! ___ Sieh, der Mor_gen däm _ _ _mert. _____

leidenschaftlich bewegt.

Flieh _ _ _ e denn aus meinen Ar _ men! ___

denn ver_säu_mest du die Zeit, möch_ten für ein kurz ___ Er_war_men wir er_

tau ___ schen lan ___ ges Leid. _____

zurückhaltend.

etwas ruhiger im Zeitmaasse.　　　　　　　　*zunehmend.*

Ist in Fe_ge_feu_ers_qua_len doch ein ___ Tag schon aus_zu_stehn, ___ wenn die

allmählig durch Zurückhalten in das Hauptzeitmaass übergehend.

Hoff_nung fern ___ in Strah_len lässt des Him ___ mels Glo ___ rie

ITALIAN SONGBOOK
ITALIENISCHES LIEDERBUCH

1. Auch kleine Dinge

Langsam und sehr zart. (♩ = 54.)

pp

p

p

p

Little things can be done too

Auch klei_ne Din _ _ ge kön_nen uns ent_zü _ cken,

immer pp

pp

auch klei_ne Din _ _ ge kön_nen theu_er sein. Be_denkt, wie gern wir_

_uns mit Per_len schmü_cken; sie wer_den schwer be_zahlt und sind nur klein.

2. Mir ward gesagt

Langsam und sehr innig. (♩ = 48.)

Mir ward ge_sagt, du rei_ _sest in die Fer_ ne.

Ach, wo_hin gehst du, mein_ ge_lieb_tes Le_ _ben? den Tag, an dem du schei_

_dest, wüsst' ich ger_ne; mit Thrä_nen will ich das Ge_leit dir ge_ben.

mit Tranen (with tears)

3. Ihr seid die Allerschönste

Innig und leidenschaftlich. (♩=100.)

Ihr seid die Al_ler_schön__ste weit und breit, viel schö_ner als im
Mai der Blu__men_flor. Or_vie_to's Dom steigt so voll Herr__lich_keit.
Vi_ter_bo's grö_ster Brun__nen nicht em_por.

4. Gesegnet sei, durch den die Welt entstund

Schif_fe, die hi_nü_ber _ glei _ ten, er schuf das Pa_ra_dies mit ew'_gem

poco cresc._ _ _ _

Licht, _____ er schuf die Schönheit und dein An _ _ _ ge_sicht.

dim. _____

5. Selig ihr Blinden

Ziemlich getragen, jedoch nicht schleppend. (♩= 56.)

Se - lig ihr Blin - den, die ihr nicht zu

schau - en ver - mögt ___ die Rei - ze, die uns Gluth ent - fa - chen; se - lig ihr

Tau - ben, die ihr oh - ne Grau - en die Kla - gen der Ver - lieb - - ten könnt ver -

la _ chen; se _ lig ihr Stum _ men, die ihr nicht den Frau _ en könnt eu _ re

Her _ zens_noth ver_ständ_lich ma _ chen; se _ lig ihr Tod _ ten, die man hat be_

gra _ ben! ihr sollt vor Lie_bes_qua _ _ len Ruh _ e ha _ _

ben.

6. Wer rief dich denn?

7. Der Mond hat eine schwere Klag' erhoben

Sehr langsam. (♩=44.)

Der Mond hat ei_ne schwe_re Klag' er_ho_ben

und vor dem Herrn die Sa _ _ che kund _ ge_macht: Er wol_le nicht mehr stehn_

_ am Him_mel dro _ ben, du ha_best ihn um sei_nen Glanz _ ge_bracht.

Als er zu-letzt das Ster - nen-heer ge-zählt, da hab' es an der vol-

-len Zahl ge-fehlt; zwei von den schön-sten ha - best du ent-wen-det:

die bei-den Au-gen dort, die mich ver-blen-det.

8. Nun lass uns Frieden schliessen

Now let us make peace, dear lit

9. Dass doch gemalt all' deine Reize wären

Im gan _ zen Lan _ _ _ de würd' es aus _ _ _ ge _ schrie _ ben,

cresc.

Erstes Zeitmass.

Christ soll' ein Je _ der wer _ den und dich

immer zurückhaltender.

ff

dim.

lie _ _ ben.

Ein je _ der Hei _ de flugs be _ kehr _ te sich

p

pp

und würd' ein gu _ ter Christ und lieb _ _ te dich.

etwas zurückhaltend.

p

dimin.

pp

ppp

10. Du denkst mit einem Fädchen mich zu fangen

du darfst mir ja nicht trau'n, siehst du mich la_chen. Schon An_ _dre fing ich,

glaub' es si _ cher_lich. Ich bin ver _ liebt, doch e_ben nicht in

dich;___ ich bin ver _ liebt, _____ doch e_ben nicht in dich.

162

11. Wie lange schon war immer mein Verlangen

How long has it been my desire

Sehr langsam und nicht ohne Humor. (♩=40.)
(gefühlvoll.)

Wie lan _ ge schon war immer mein Ver _ lan _ gen: ach, _ wä _ re doch ein Mu _ si _ kus mir gut! Nun _ liess der Herr mich _ meinen Wunsch er _ lan _ gen und schickt mir ei _ nen, ganz wie

milk and roses

Milch und Blut. Da kommt er e _ ben her mit

12. Nein, junger Herr

Lebhaft und mit Grazie. (♩=152.)

Nein, jun_ger Herr, so treibt man's nicht, für wahr; man sorgt da_

für, sich schick_ _lich zu be_tra_gen. Für All_tags bin ich

gut ge_nug, nicht wahr? Doch Bess_re suchst du dir an Fei_ _er_

ta _ _ gen. _____

immer zurückhaltender _ _ _ _ _ _

Nein, jun _ ger Herr, wirst du so wei _ ter sünd' _ gen, wird dir den

langsam. *rasch.*

Dienst dein All _ _ _ tags _ lieb _ chen künd' _ gen.

13. Hoffährtig seid Ihr, schönes Kind

14. Geselle, woll'n wir uns in Kutten hüllen

15. Mein Liebster ist so klein

My (true) love is too small

Mässig, nicht zu schnell. (♩=104.)

(sehr zart)

Mein Lieb-ster ist so klein, dass oh-ne

without bending he sweeps the floor with his hair/locks/curls

Bü-cken ___ er mir das Zim-mer fegt ___ mit sei-nen Lo-cken.

Als er in's Gärt-lein ging, ___ Jas-min zu pflü-cken, ist er vor ei-ner Schne-

16. Ihr jungen Leute

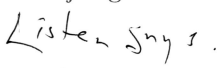

Lasst nie ihn un_ter frei_em Himmel schla_fen; er ist so

zart, es möch_te sich be_stra_fen. Lasst mir ihn ja nicht schla_fen un_term

Mond; er gin_ge drauf, er ist's ja nicht ge_wohnt.

17. Und willst du deinen Liebsten sterben sehen

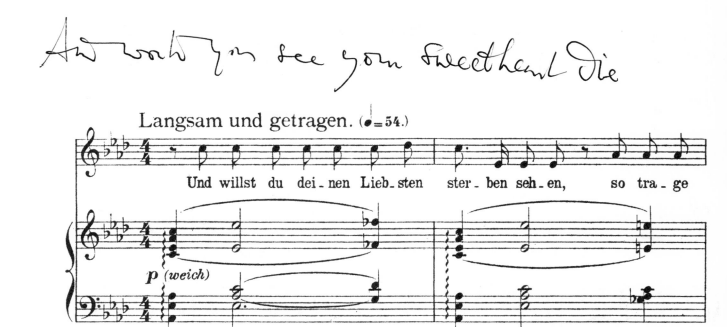

Das Lied ist auch mit Orchester erschienen;
Orchesterbegleitung von Max Reger.
The song has also been arranged for orchestra by Max Reger.

sehr ruhig. (♩=44.)

Wie gold_ne Fä _ _ den, die der Wind be _ wegt

schön sind die Haa _ re, schön _____ ist, die sie trägt!

Gold _ fä _ _ den, Sei _ den _ fä _ den un _ _ ge_zählt —

schön sind die Haa _ re, schön ist, die sie strählt!

18. Heb' auf dein blondes Haupt

Das er_ste: dass um dich mein Her_ze bricht,___

das zweite: dir nur will ich an_ge_hö_ren,

das drit_te: dass ich dir mein Heil be_feh___le,

(zart.)

das letz_te: dich al_lein ___ liebt mei_ne See_le.

sehr zart.

19. Wir haben Beide lange Zeit geschwiegen

wie - der. Die En - gel Got - tes sind he - rab - ge - flo - gen, mit ih - nen

ist der Frie - den ein - ge - zo - gen. Die Lie - bes - en - gel ka - men ü - ber

Nacht und ha - ben Frie - den mei - ner Brust ge - bracht.

20. Mein Liebster singt am Haus

Strom am Bett hab ich ge - weint, _____ weiss nicht vor Thrä _ _ _ nen,

ob der Mor _ gen scheint. Den breiten Strom am Bett weint' ich vor

Seh _ nen; blind ha_ben mich gemacht die blut'_ _ gen Thrä_nen.

21. Man sagt mir, deine Mutter woll' es nicht

Stil - len! Nein, mein Ge - - lieb - ter, folg' ihr nim - mer - mehr,

thu's ihr zum Trotz, komm öf - ter als bis - her! Nein, hö - re — nicht auf

sie, was — sie auch sa - ge; thu's ihr zum Trotz, mein Lieb, komm

al - - - - - - - - - - le Ta - ge!

22. Ein Ständchen Euch zu bringen

dass am Tag, der vier _ _ _ _ _ und _ zwan _ zig zählt, _____ sie

immer zurückhaltend. _ _ _ _ _ _ _ _ _ _ _

fünf _ _ _ _ und _ zwan _ zig Stun _ _ den lang mir

lebhaft.

fehlt. _____

nachlassend.

23. Was für ein Lied soll dir gesungen werden

What kind of song could I sing you

Sehr ruhig. (♩ = 54)

(ausdrucksvoll)

Was für ein Lied soll dir ge-sun-gen wer-den, das dei- -ner

how can I find it

wür- -dig sei? Wo find' ich's nur? Am lieb-sten grüb' ich es

tief aus der Er - - den, ge-sun - - gen noch von kei-ner Cre-a - tur. __

Ein Lied, das we-der Mann noch Weib bis heu - te hört' o - der sang, selbst

nicht die ält'-sten Leu - te.

24. Ich esse nun mein Brod nicht trocken mehr

I don't eat my bread anymore

Ziemlich langsam. (♩ = 60)

Ich esse nun mein Brod nicht trocken mehr,*)

ein Dorn ist mir im

a thorn has lodged in my foot   in vain (I'm looking)

Fu-sse stecken blieben.   Umsonst   nach rechts und links ___ blick' ich um-

left & right   and found no one to love

her,   und Keinen find' ich, der mich möchte lie-ben.

poco ritard.

dim. — pp

*) nämlich: mit Thränen befeuchtet.

Gemächlich.

Wenn's doch auch nur ein al - tes Männlein wä - re, das ___ mir er-zeigt' ein

we-nig Lieb' und Eh - re. Ich mei-ne nämlich, so ein wohl-ge-stal-ter, ehr - ba-rer

immer etwas zurückhaltend

Greis, et - wa von meinem Al-ter. Ich mei-ne, um mich ganz zu of-fen-ba-ren,

a tempo   *lebhafter*

ein al-tes Männlein ___ so ___ von vierzehn Jah - ren.

25. Mein Liebster hat zu Tische mich geladen

und zum Bra - - ten, der Ha - fen auch war längst ent - zwei ge - gan - gen.

An ei - nem Fäss - chen Wein_ ge - brach es auch, und

Glä - ser hatt' er gar nicht im Ge - brauch; der Tisch war schmal, das

riten. a tempo

Ta - feltuch nicht bes - ser, das Brot steinhart und völ - lig stumpf das Messer.

26. Ich liess mir sagen und mir ward erzählt

(I was told, and it was related)

dau-ung stählt,   ver-speis't er ei - ne Wurst und sie - - ben Bro-de,

und lindert nicht To - ni - - na sei - ne Pein,   bricht nächstens Hungersnoth und

Theu-rung ein.

27. Schon streckt' ich aus im Bett

Ich sing' und spie-le, dass die Stra-sse schallt; so Man-che lauscht

p (dolce)   *pp*

vor - ü-ber bin ich bald. So manches Mädchen hat mein Lied ge-rührt,

p

pp

in - dess der Wind schon Sang___ und Klang ent-führt.

pp

pp   *ppp*   *pp*   *ppp*

28. Du sagst mir, dass ich keine Fürstin sei

You tell me I'm no Queen.

but neither are you descended from the Spanish throne

Langsam und breit. (♩ = 66)

Du sagst mir, dass ich kei - ne Für - - stin sei;

auch du bist nicht auf Spaniens Thron entsprossen. Nein, Bester, stehst du

auf — bei Hahnenschrei, fährst du aufs Feld und nicht in Staats - karossen.

Du spot-test mein um mei-ne Nie-drig-keit,

doch Ar- -muth thut dem

(sehr ausdrucksvoll)

A-del nichts zu Leid.

Du spottest, dass mir Kro-ne fehlt und Wappen,

und fährst doch selber nur mit Schusters Rappen.

29. Wohl kenn' ich Eueren Stand

Män-ner leicht besieg-tet Ihr, drum weiss ich wohl, Ihr treibt nur Spiel mit mir.

Ihr spottet mein, man hat mich war - nen wol-len, doch ach, Ihr seid so schön!

Wer kann Euch grol - len?

(sehr ausdrucksvoll)

poco ritard.

30. Lass sie nur gehn, die so die Stolze spielt

Sehr mässig. (♩ = 72)

Lass sie nur gehn, die so die Stolze spielt, das Wunderkräutlein aus dem Blu-menfeld.

Man sieht, wo-hin ihr blan-kes Au-ge zielt, da Tag um Tag ein An- -drer ihr gefällt.

Sie treibt es gra-de wie Tos-

ca - na's Fluss, dem je-des Berg-ge-wäs - - ser fol - gen muss.

poco a poco cresc.

Sie treibt es wie der Ar - no, will mir scheinen:

bald hat sie viel Be- -wer-ber, bald nicht Einen. *)

etwas breiter

poco rit.

dim. - - - *pp*

*) Wie in den heissen Sommermonaten den Arno seine Nebenflüsse im Stich lassen.

31. Wie soll ich fröhlich sein

Mässig. (♩ = 76)

Wie soll ich fröh-lich sein und la-chen gar, da du mir im-mer zür-

poco riten.   etwas bewegt (♩ = 88)

nest un-ver-ho-len? Du kommst nur Ein-mal al-le hundert Jahr, und dann,

als hätte man dir's an be-foh-len. Was kommst du, wenn's die Deinen un-gern

sehn? Gieb frei mein Herz, dann magst du wei - ter gehn.

Daheim mit deinen Leu - - ten leb' in Frie - den, denn was der Himmel will,

I. Zeitmass.

geschieht hie - nie - - den. Halt Frie - den mit den Dei - ni - gen zu Haus,

denn was der Himmel will, das bleibt nicht aus.

32. Was soll der Zorn, mein Schatz

Und taugt ein Mes-ser nicht, so nimm ein Schwert, dass meines Blu-tes Quell

p f p

—gen Him - mel fährt. Und taugt ein Schwert nicht, nimm des Dol - -ches Stahl

f p

und wasch' in mei-nem Blut all mei - ne Qual.

f più f ff

sf p dim. sf

33. Sterb' ich, so hüllt in Blumen meine Glieder

se-hen habt. Dort legt mich hin in Re-gen o-der Wind;

gern sterb' ich, ist's um dich, ge-lieb-tes Kind. Dort legt mich hin in Son-nen-

schein und Re-gen; ich ster-be lieb-lich, sterb' ich

dei-net-we-gen.

pp

34. Und steht Ihr früh am Morgen auf

Und steht Ihr früh am Morgen auf vom Bette, scheucht Ihr vom Himmel al - le Wol - ken fort, die Son - ne lockt Ihr auf die Ber - ge dort, und En - gelein er - schei - nen um die Wet - te, und brin - gen Schuh und Klei - der Euch sofort. Dann, wenn Ihr ausgeht in die

heil' - ge Met-te, so zieht Ihr al - le Men - - schen mit Euch fort,

und wenn Ihr naht der be-ne-dei-ten Stät-te, so zün-det Eu-er Blick die Lam - pen

an. Weihwasser nehmt Ihr, macht des Kreuzez Zei - chen und netzet Eu-re weisse

Stirn so-dann und nei - get Euch und beugt die Knie in-glei-chen

o wie hold-se - lig steht Euch al - les an! Wie hold___ und se - lig

hat Euch Gott begabt, die Ihr der Schönheit Kron'___ em-pfan-gen habt!

Wie hold und se - lig wan - - delt Ihr im Le - ben; der Schönheit Pal-me ward an

Euch ge-ge-ben.

35. Benedeit die sel'ge Mutter

Wenn ich aus der Fer-ne schmachte und be-trach-te dei-ne Schö-ne,

p poco a poco cresc.- - - - - - - - - - - -

sie-he wie ich beb', und stöhne, dass ich kaum es ber - -gen kann!

f   p   f   p   f   dim.   p

leidenschaftlich und etwas drängend   *immer zurückhaltender*

und in mei-ner Brust ge - waltsam fühl' ich Flammen sich em - pö-ren, die den Frieden mir zer-

p   *molto* cre - -scen - -do   f

langsam   I. Zeitmass.

stören, ach, der Wahnsinn fasst mich an!

ff   p   mf   p   mf   dimin.

Be-ne-deit die sel'-ge Mut-ter, die so lieb - - lich dich gebo-ren,

so an Schönheit aus-er-ko-ren___ mei-ne Sehn-sucht fliegt dir zu! du so

lieb-lich von Ge-ber-den, du___ die Hol - de-ste der Er - den, du mein Klei-nod,

mei-ne Won - ne, Sü - sse, be - ne - deit___ bist du!

36. Wenn Du, mein Liebster, steigst zum Himmel auf

etwas bewegter

Und sieht der Herr-gott uns're Lie-bes-schmer - - zen,

mit immer gesteigertem Ausdruck

macht er Ein Herz aus zwei ver-lieb-ten Her - zen, zu Ei - nem Her-zen

immer zurückhaltender

fügt er zwei zu-sam-men, im Pa-ra-dies, um-glänzt von Himmelsflam - men.

viel bewegter   *immer zurückhaltender   I. Zeitmass.*

37. Wie viele Zeit verlor ich, dich zu lieben!

Sehr gehalten. (♩ = 52)

Wie vie-le Zeit verlor ich, dich zu lie-ben!

hätt' ich doch Gott geliebt___ in all der Zeit. Ein Platz im Pa-ra-dies___

___ wär' mir ver-schrie-ben, ein Heil'-ger säs-se dann___ an mei-ner Seit'.

38. Wenn du mich mit den Augen streifst und lachst

39. Gesegnet sei das Grün

Ge-seg-net sei das Grün und wer es trägt! Ein grü-nes Kleid will ich mir ma-chen las-sen. Ein grü-nes Kleid trägt auch die Früh-lings-au-e. Grün klei-det sich der Lieb - ling mei-ner Au - gen.

In Grün __ sich klei-den ist der Jä-ger Brauch, ein grü-nes Kleid trägt __

__ mein Gelieb-ter auch; das Grün steht al-len Din-gen lieb-lich an,

aus Grün __ wächst je-de schö-ne Frucht __ her-an.

40. O wär' dein Haus durchsichtig wie ein Glas

41. Heut Nacht erhob ich mich um Mitternacht

Ziemlich langsam. ♩=50.

Heut Nacht er-hob ich mich um Mit-ternacht, da

war___ mein Herz___ mir heim - lich fort-geschlichen. Ich frug: Herz, wohin stürmst du so mit Macht?

es sprach: Nur Euch zu sehn, sei es ent-wichen. Nun sieh, wie muss es um mein Lie - ben stehn:

mein Herz entweicht der Brust,___ um dich zu sehn.

42. Nicht länger kann ich singen

Langsam und recht kläglich vorzutragen. ♩=86.

Nicht län-ger kann ich sin-gen, denn der Wind weht stark und macht dem

A - them was zu schaf-fen. Auch fürcht' ich, dass die Zeit um-sonst ver-rinnt.

Ja wär' ich si-cher, ging' ich jetzt nicht schla - fen. Ja wüsst' ich was,

würd' ich nicht heim spazieren und ein-sam die-se schö-ne Zeit verlie - ren.

43. Schweig' einmal still

Schweig' einmal still, du garst'ger Schwätzer dort! Zum E - kel ist mir dein verwünsch - tes Singen. Und triebst du es bis mor -

- gen früh so fort, doch wür-de dir kein schmu-ckes Lied ge-lin-gen.

Schweig' _____ ein-mal still und le - ge dich auf's Ohr! _____

_____ Das Ständchen ei-nes E - - - sels zög' ich vor.

44. O wüsstest du, wie viel ich deinetwegen

Sehr mässig und ja nicht eilen. (♪ = 108.)

O wüsstest du, wie viel ich dei-net-we-gen, du falsche Re-ne-ga-tin,

litt zur Nacht, in-dess du im ver-schlossnen Haus ge-le - gen

und ich die Zeit im Frei - - en zu-ge-bracht.

Als Ro - sen-was-ser dien-te mir der Re - gen,

der Blitz hat Lie-bes-bot - schaft mir ge-bracht; ich ha-be Wür-fel mit dem

Sturm ge-spielt, als un-ter dei-nem Dach ich Wa - - che hielt.

Mein Bett war un-ter dei-nem Dach be-rei-tet, der

Him - mel lag als De - - cke drauf ge - brei - tet, die Schwelle dei - ner Thür, _

_ die war mein Kis - sen _ ich Ärm - ster, ach, _ was hab' ich

aus - - steh'n müs - sen!

234

45. Verschling' der Abgrund meines Liebsten Hütte

Drin hause ei - ne Schlan - - ge, gift - ge -

schwol - len, und bring' ihm

Tod,_____ der mich ver-ra - then wollen!

46. Ich hab' in Penna einen Liebsten wohnen

und wie-der ei-nen hab' ich in Ma - gio - - - ne,

vier in La Fratta, zehn __ in Castig-lio - - ne.